What Do I Want? What Do I Need?

Rachel Eagen

Crabtree Publishing Company
www.crabtreebooks.com

Money Sense
An Introduction to Financial Literacy

Author: Rachel Eagen

Series research and development: Reagan Miller

Editors: Reagan Miller and Janine Deschenes

Designer: Tammy McGarr

Photo research: Tammy McGarr and Crystal Sikkens

Proofreader: Crystal Sikkens

Prepress technician: Tammy McGarr

Print and production coordinator: Katherine Berti

Photographs

iStock: © andresr: p 20

Shutterstock: © Valentina Razumova: pp 4, 21 (game system);
    © Diana Beato: p 12; © Rob Wilson: p 21 (right middle);

Thinkstock: moodboard: p 15

All other images from Shutterstock

Library and Archives Canada Cataloguing in Publication

Eagen, Rachel, 1979-, author
    What do I want? what do I need? / Rachel Eagen.

(Money sense : an introduction to financial literacy)
Includes index.
Issued in print and electronic formats.
ISBN 978-0-7787-2664-7 (hardback).--
ISBN 978-0-7787-2668-5 (paperback).--
ISBN 978-1-4271-1800-4 (html)

    1. Finance, Personal--Juvenile literature. 2. Consumption
(Economics)--Juvenile literature. I. Title.

HG179.E221 2016   j332.024   C2016-904167-0
                                           C2016-904168-9

Library of Congress Cataloging-in-Publication Data

CIP available at the Library of Congress

Crabtree Publishing Company

Printed in Canada/082016/TL20160715

www.crabtreebooks.com   1-800-387-7650

Published in Canada
Crabtree Publishing
616 Welland Ave.
St. Catharines, Ontario
L2M 5V6

Published in the United States
Crabtree Publishing
PMB 59051
350 Fifth Avenue, 59th Floor
New York, New York 10118

Published in the United Kingdom
Crabtree Publishing
Maritime House
Basin Road North, Hove
BN41 1WR

Published in Australia
Crabtree Publishing
3 Charles Street
Coburg North
VIC 3058

Table of Contents

Money Everywhere

People spend money almost every day. They buy food at grocery stores. They buy toys and clothes at shopping malls. Some things people buy are **needs**. Other things they buy are **wants**.

To make good decisions about money, we need to decide whether something is a want or a need.

Making good decisions

People need money to buy the things they need and want, but we do not have an endless supply of money. That means that people have to make good **decisions** as to how they spend their money.

5

What are Needs?

A need is something that a person must have to be healthy and safe. Our needs include things such as food, fresh air, shelter, clothing, and exercise. Many of our needs cost money to buy, such as food and clothing. A few of our needs do not cost money, such as fresh air and exercise.

Playing outside with our friends does not cost money. This is one way we can meet our needs for fresh air and exercise.

Same need, different ways

People have the same needs, but we may meet them in different ways. For example, we all need shelter. To meet this need, some families live in apartment buildings, while others live in houses.

We all have a need for food. Some people might choose to meet this need by eating at a restaurant, while others might cook their food at home.

What are Wants?

A want is something that we would like to have. Some examples of wants are junk food, video games, and toys. Wants can also be activities, such as visiting the zoo or taking guitar lessons.

People have different wants, but everyone has the same needs. Which things on this page are needs, and which are wants?

Your wants could be the same or different from the wants of your friends and family.

What do you want?

Many of our wants cost money, such as going to the movies, or getting a new comic book. Some of our wants do not cost money, such as visiting the park or walking your dog. Everyone has different wants, because we all want different things.

Knowing the Difference

"I need that!" Have you ever said those words? Sometimes, we think we need things when we really just want them. It's normal to want what other people have, but no one can **afford** to buy everything they want. We have to learn the difference between wants and needs.

Make "**cents**" of it!

We need food to survive, but not all kinds of food are needs. We need foods that help keep us healthy and strong.

Look at the list below. Which types of foods are needs, and which are not?

- **Fruit, such as apples, oranges, and bananas**
- **Ice cream**
- **Chocolate bars**

What is the difference?

It can be hard to tell the difference between wants and needs, especially when we really want something. At school, you might notice a friend's new backpack, and wish you had one, too. But chances are, you already have your own backpack, and don't need a new one.

Smart Spending

Advertisements by different companies can make us think we need something when we really don't. They might show famous people using the product or show happy people having fun while using the product. The point of these advertisements is to push us to buy their products.

Companies advertise on television, the radio, and the Internet. You might even see advertisements along streets in big cities.

Tough choices

It is important to make smart choices when buying products. We must think about whether we are buying a product because of an advertisement, or because we really need it. Sometimes advertisements for popular **brands** might make it seem like their product is better than the rest, but these popular brands often cost more money.

When buying a product, we must decide if the popular brand is worth the extra money, or if a cheaper brand that is not as well known is just as good.

13

Wanting More than you Need

People can only buy what they can afford, or pay for. We do not have an unlimited supply of money. People have to **earn** money by doing **jobs**. Then, they can spend the money they earn.

Have you ever bought something using money you earned yourself?

14

Making choices

Sometimes people want more than they can afford. When this happens, they need to make choices. You really want to buy a new pair of roller blades. However, you promised your sister you would pay half the cost of your Dad's birthday present. You really want the roller blades, but you should save your money for your Dad's present.

Sometimes you have to decide what is more important to spend your money on.

Making Good Choices

People need to make good choices when deciding how to spend their money. They must meet all of their needs to survive. When people earn money, they have to spend it on needs first.

Healthy foods are a need.

After people have paid for their needs, they might choose to spend their extra money on a new car or televsion.

Needs first, wants second

If money is left over after paying for needs, people can choose to spend it on wants. Making good choices helps people meet all of their needs, and get some of their wants.

Decision Making

Making good choices means that you have to decide whether or not it is a good idea to buy something. It can help to think about the pros and cons, or **advantages** and **disadvantages**, before making a purchase.

Make "cents" of it!

Making a chart can help you look at the pros and cons of buying a want. Look at this chart. Do you think that buying new running shoes would be a good choice?

Pros/Advantages

- My old shoes hurt my feet
- I can afford them because I saved up the money I got for my birthday

Cons/Disadvantages

- I won't have money left over to buy chocolate milk at lunch this week

Think about it

Before you choose to buy something, think about why you want it. Do you need it? How much money do you have to spend, and how much does it cost? Can you afford to buy it? How much money will you have left over to save or spend on other things?

Making a Budget

A budget is a plan for using money. It is an **estimate** of how much money someone has, and how much they will need to spend, for a set period of time. People use budgets to make sure they have enough money to buy the things they need.

Budgets help prevent people from **overspending** their money.

Using a budget

Your parents might estimate that they need to spend 300 dollars every month on groceries. They would use a budget to make sure they have 300 dollars available every month to spend on this need.

Make "cents" of it!

Imagine you are in charge of your family's budget. What would you spend your money on first? What things would you buy only if you had money left over? Explain your thinking.

Learning More

Books

Drobot, Eve. *Money Money Money: Where It Comes From, How to Save It, Spend It, and Make It.* Toronto: Maple Tree Press Inc. 2004.

Hall, Margaret. *Money: Earning, Saving, Spending.* Chicago: Heinemann. 2008.

Kemper, Bitsy. *Budgeting, Spending, and Saving.* Minneapolis: Lerner Publications. 2015.

Websites

Social Studies for Kids
www.socialstudiesforkids.com/articles/economics/ wantsandneeds1.htm

Rich Kid Smart Kid
www.richkidsmartkid.com

The United States Mint: H.I.P. Pocket Change
www.usmint.gov/kids

Sense and Dollars
www.senseanddollars.thinkport.org

Words to Know

advantage (ad-VAN-tij) noun Something that helps you do well

advertisement (ad-ver-TAHYZ-muhnt) noun An announcement of goods for sale

afford (uh-FAWRD) verb To have enough money to buy or do something

brand (brand) noun Products made by a particular company

decision (dih-SIZH-uhn) noun To make a choice after careful thought

disadvantage (dis-uhd-VAN-tij) noun Something that does not help you do well

earn (urn) verb To receive money for performing a task

estimate (ES-tuh-mit) noun An opinion of how much something will probably cost

job (job) noun A task done for a set amount of money

need (need) noun Something a person must have to be healthy and safe

overspending (oh-ver-SPEND-ing) verb To spend more money than you should

survive (ser-VAHYV) verb To stay alive

want (wont) noun Something a person would like to have but does not need

A noun is a person, place, or thing.

A verb is an action word that tells you what someone or something does.

23

Index

About the Author

Rachel Eagen studied Creative Writing and English Literature at university. Now, she edits and writes books for a living. She is the author of 17 other books for children and youth. She plans to put the money she earned from writing this book into her what-if fund.